BOYS IN THE GOOD

THE GOOD BOOK

A KID'S GUIDE TO BECOMING A SUCCESSFUL STUDENT LEADER

BY DA'NALL WILMER
ILLUSTRATED BY CAMERON WILSON

The Good Book: A Kid's Guide to Becoming a Successful Student Leader

Copyright © 2018 by Da'Nall Wilmer

All rights reserved. This book or any portion thereof may not be reproduced or used in any manner whatsoever without the express written permission of the publisher except for the use of brief quotations in a book review.

Printed by CreateSpace, an Amazon.com company

First Printing, 2018

ISBN 978-0692155912

www.boysinthegood.com

Dedicated to "Boys in the Good" and the many students who I have had the honor of teaching and mentoring. Impacting your life has changed mine.
- *Mr. Wilmer*

Being a kid, these days is not as easy as it seems;
We have our future goals and even bigger dreams.
Many kids our age have important shoes to fill,
Like being a student leader --- which requires a major skill.

No matter what goals we have when we grow into adults,
Being a good leader will always bring about good results.
What better time for us to make a change than now?
There are four key aims that will certainly show us how.

Meet Carter, Deshaun, Jai'ree and Mekhi.
Look closely, they're all well-dressed, with each in a tie.
A good first impression is impressive, as you can see.
Professional appearance is great, but what you have inside is key.

GIVING

The first aim is GIVING --- have you heard of this before?
Like being a gentleman and holding open a door.
Giving back to those who may have less than you
Will make you feel much better about your own life too.

Carter helps with the food drive at his school each year.
He always supports his teammates with a loud and prideful cheer.

When a new student arrived, and had not much to say, Carter welcomed them at recess and asked if they would play.

Here's the part about giving that every kid should learn:
People who earnestly give expect nothing in return.
Being a good leader could be simple if you try.
But that's not all it takes, and Deshaun will show you why.

OPTIMISM

OPTIMISM is the second aim that every kid should know.
It means having a positive attitude even when things seem low.
Trying your best to smile each day and focusing on the good
Will make you feel much better, as Deshaun once understood.

When things just didn't seem quite right one afternoon at school,
He didn't once complain and that made him feel really cool.
He let his failures motivate him and worked harder to improve
When he didn't get a good math grade that his father would approve.

Negative thoughts may set in when things don't go our way,
But good leaders should be positive and mind what they say.
Deshaun always tells himself that things will be just fine.
Even when it rains outside, the sun will sooner or later shine.

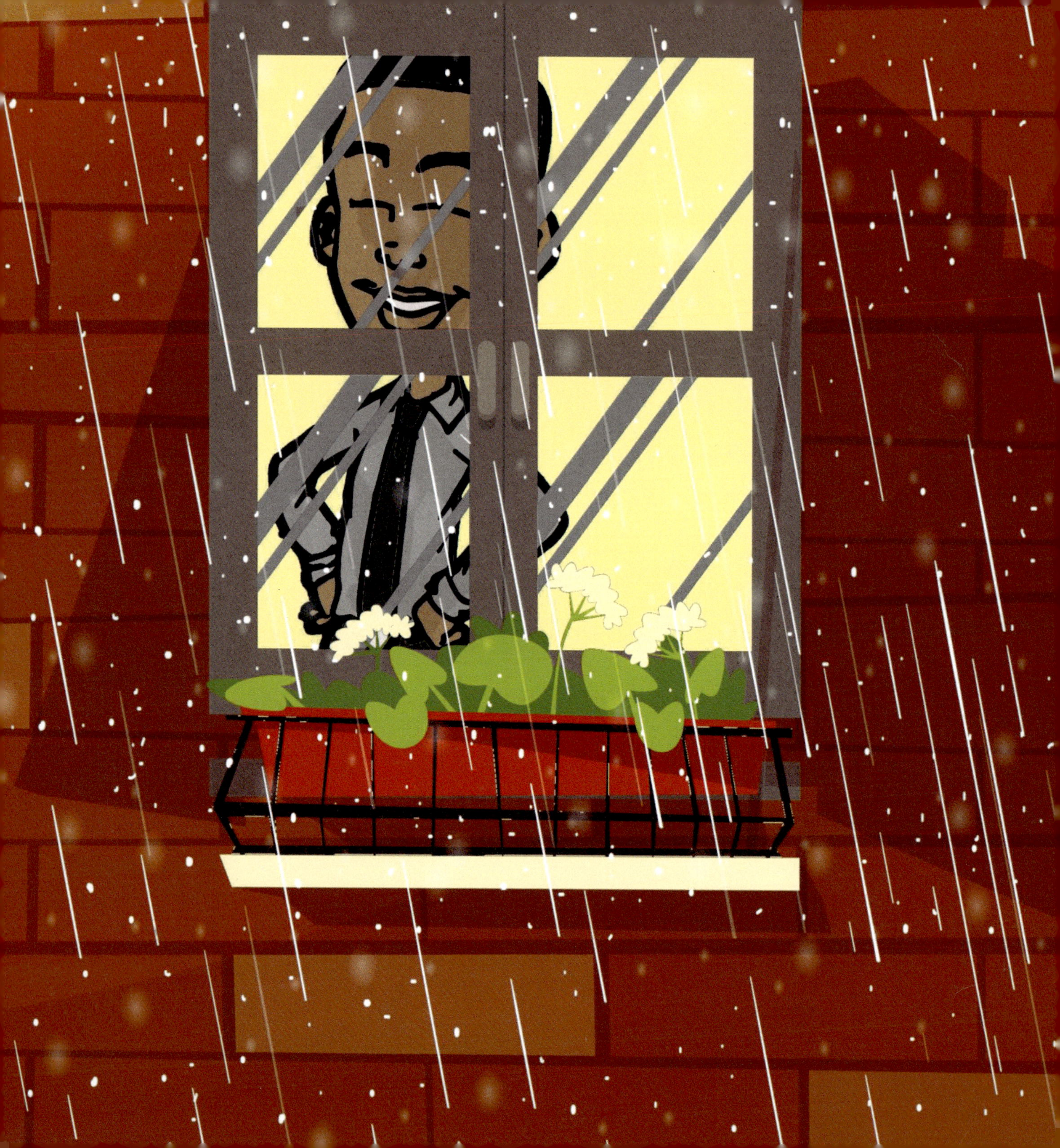

ORIGINALITY

Remember when you met Jai'ree, he had on a tie?
That's because he's a student leader and he's also pretty fly.
Standing out from the crowd while others act the same
Is the reason why ORIGINALITY is the next and third aim.

Many kids today will do whatever it takes to fit in.
Why not try something new and set a unique and positive trend?
Many kids don't know that they can be great role models too.
So, set a good example and mentor a kid who is younger than you.

Instead of making bad decisions on the way home from school, Jai'ree left his friends and went home to obey his parents' every rule. Recognizing your "real" friends is what good leadership is about. Ask yourself, why fit in when you were born to stand out?

DETERMINATION

The final aim to share with you will put you to the test. It is called DETERMINATION, and it's just as important as the rest. Keep your focus on your goals even when things seem tough. Good leaders try their hardest, and never give up, though the challenges may be rough.

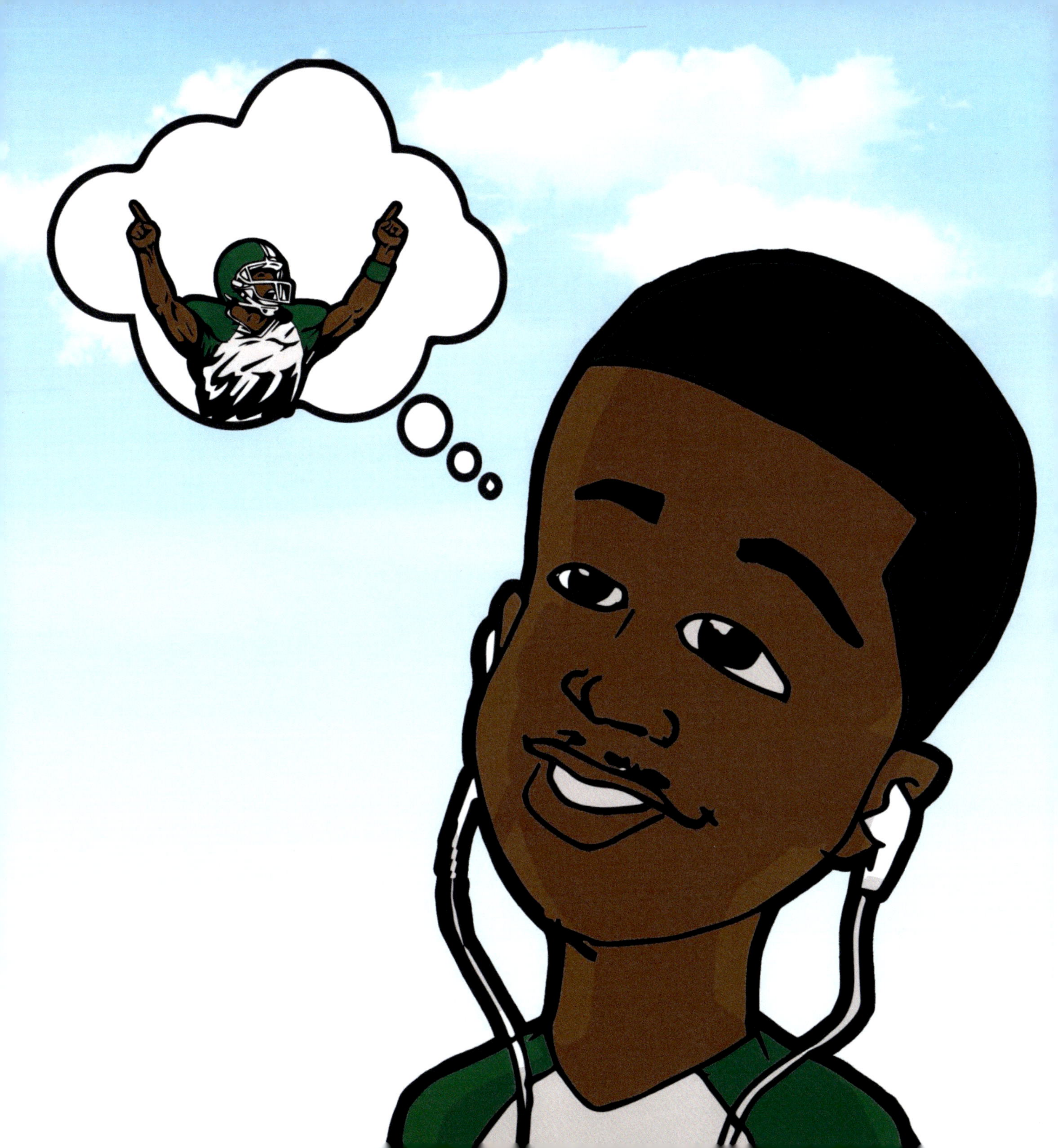

Mekhi has many dreams and aspirations that he'd love to fulfill;
Like growing up to be a football player with each amazing skill.
Mekhi knows it is valuable to have a backup plan,
So, he studies hard and practices football, as often as he can.

CHEMISTRY

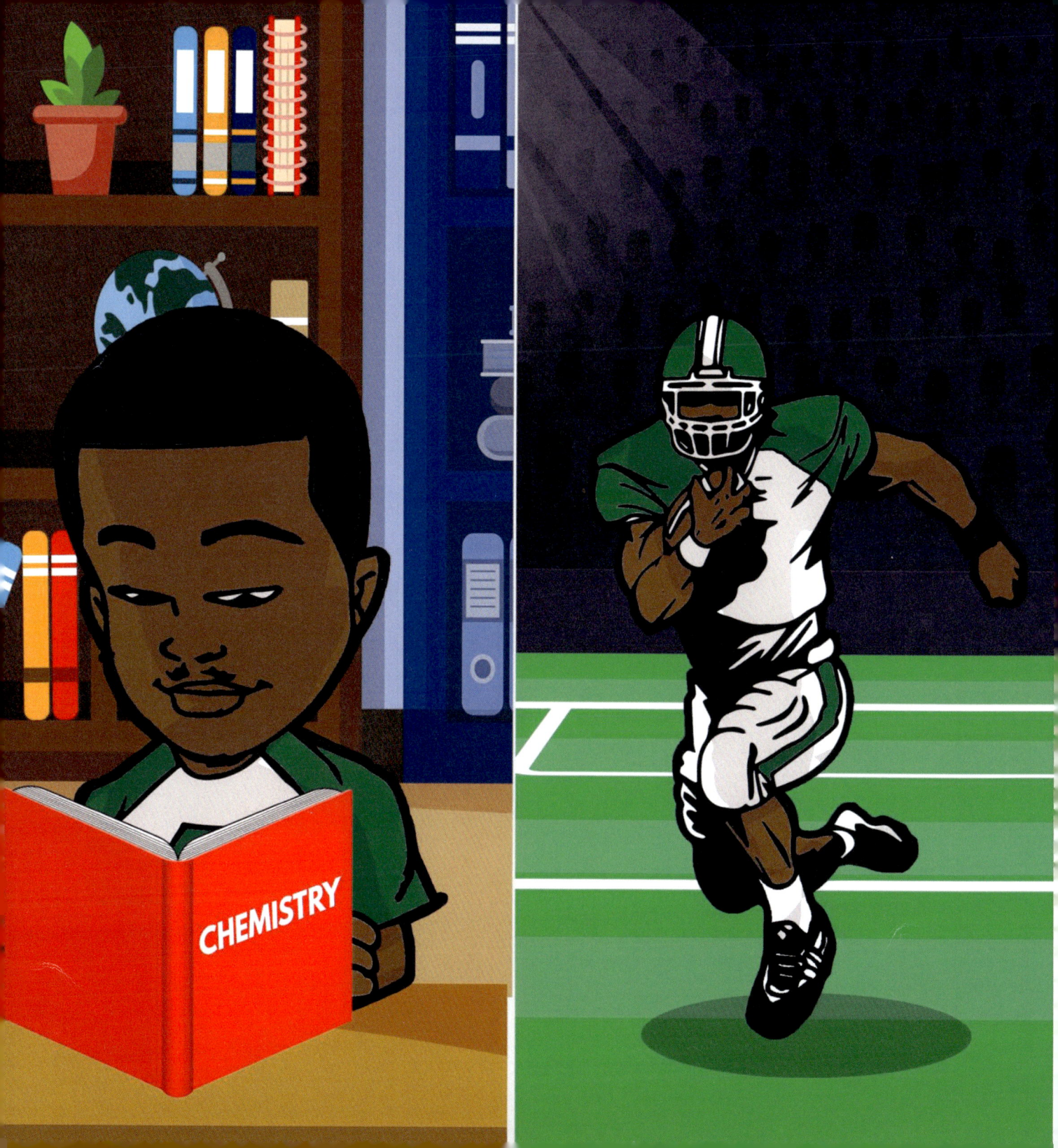

Student leaders strive for excellence and always set a high goal.
The key is challenging yourself,
and that's what good leaders know.
Striving to excel in your studies first is very important without
a doubt.
That is what determination is really all about.

There's no better time for you to prepare for what is next.
The choices we make and actions we take all have great effects.
Giving, Optimism, Originality, and Determination...
Are aims that are important for kids like us all across the nation.

What are your goals, dreams and big plans for tomorrow?
Try becoming a successful leader and the rest will surely follow.
Kids have the power to change the world just like adults could.
Leadership changed our lives and that's what makes us "Boys in the Good."

Made in the USA
Middletown, DE
19 February 2019